DATE DUE		

**921
DUN**

C_i

3 24571 0900463 4
Savage, Jeff.

Tim Duncan

Tim Duncan

By Jeff Savage

AMAZING ATHLETES

Lerner Publications Company • Minneapolis

Copyright © 2010 by Jeff Savage

All rights reserved. International copyright secured. No part of this book may be reproduced, stored in a retrieval system, or transmitted in any form or by any means—electronic, mechanical, photocopying, recording, or otherwise—without the prior written permission of Lerner Publishing Group, Inc., except for the inclusion of brief quotations in an acknowledged review.

Lerner Publications Company
A division of Lerner Publishing Group, Inc.
241 First Avenue North
Minneapolis, MN 55401 U.S.A.

Website address: www.lernerbooks.com

Library of Congress Cataloging-in-Publication Data

Savage, Jeff, 1961–
    Tim Duncan / by Jeff Savage.
        p.   cm. — (Amazing athletes)
    Includes index.
    ISBN: 978-0-8225-9993-7 (lib. bdg. : alk. paper)
    1. Duncan, Tim, 1976-—Juvenile literature. 2. Basketball players—United States—Biography—
Juvenile literature. I. Title.
    GV884.D86S26 2010
    796.323092—dc22 [B]   2008050205

Manufactured in the United States of America
1 2 3 4 5 6 – BP – 15 14 13 12 11 10

TABLE OF CONTENTS

Tim passes the ball.

THE BIG FUNDAMENTAL

Tim Duncan stood tall near the basket to receive the pass. He spun toward the hoop and banked in a shot. Seconds later, he had the ball again. Three **defenders** ran toward him. Tim smartly passed to teammate Manu Ginobili for a **three-point basket**.

The San Antonio Spurs were playing the New Orleans Hornets in the 2008 National Basketball Association (NBA) **playoffs**. The Spurs and Hornets had each won three games of this series. The team that won this seventh and final game would go to the next round of the playoffs.

Manu Ginobili jumps for a shot.

Tim *(center)* reaches for a rebound.

Tim moved his nearly seven-foot, 260-pound body near the basket again. The Hornets **fouled** him. Tim calmly sank both **free throws**. The Hornets missed a shot. Tim pulled down the **rebound**. At the other end of the floor, he made a **layup**.

Tim knew how to play in these important games. He had led San Antonio to the NBA Finals in 1999, 2003, 2005, and 2007. The Spurs won those four titles. Tim was named Finals Most Valuable Player (MVP) three times.

The Spurs led by four points late in the first half. The fans at New Orleans Arena were loud. Tim kept his cool. He lofted a shot while falling away from the basket. Swish! The Hornets followed with a free throw. The Spurs had the ball again. Tony Parker passed to Tim. Three Hornets swarmed him. Tim looked for help. He spotted Ginobili. Tim whipped a pass to Ginobili, who made a three-pointer. The lead was eight points. Tim raced down the court to play defense. The Hornets missed a shot. Tim gobbled up the rebound. The Spurs were in control.

Tim was named NBA Finals Most Valuable Player in 1999, 2003, and 2005. He joined Michael Jordan, Magic Johnson, and Shaquille O'Neal as the only players in history to win the award three times.

Tim is a skilled shooter.

Tim's nickname is the Big Fundamental. His playing style does not include fancy spins or flashy **dunks**. Instead, he makes all the right moves. He shoots with either hand. He **boxes out** for rebounds. He is a force in the **low post**. Basic basketball skills are called fundamentals. Tim uses them all. "Tim can score, rebound, block shots, everything," says Parker. "But he's unselfish enough to trust his teammates. He knows he can't win by himself."

With just over one minute left in the game, the Spurs had a slim lead. Jannero Pargo missed a three-pointer for New Orleans. Tim snared the rebound and passed the ball up the court. Parker nailed a big shot. The Hornets could not catch up. Pargo missed once more with 20 seconds left. Tim pulled down his 14th rebound of the game. The Spurs won, 91–82. "We really believed we had a chance to win on the road here," Tim said. "It's just a lot of confidence. That's what this team is all about."

Tim celebrates the Spurs' win over the Hornets.

The town of Christiansted has a harbor where ships stop to dock.

Good, Better, Best

Timothy Theodore Duncan was born April 25, 1976, on the island of Saint Croix in the Caribbean Sea. Saint Croix is the largest of the United States Virgin Islands. It is about 1,100 miles from Florida.

Tim lived with his family in a small house in Christiansted. Tim and his father, Bill, built more rooms onto the house. Tim helped his father measure every board and hammer every nail.

Tim was a bright student in school. His favorite subject was math. He was so smart that he skipped third grade. Tim and his two older sisters, Cheryl and Tricia, competed in swimming. Cheryl was a championship swimmer before she became a nurse. Tricia was a member of the U.S. Virgin Islands swim team at the 1988 Olympic Games.

Tim's mother, Ione, drove her children to swim meets. She cheered so loudly that Tim was embarrassed. "She was my biggest fan," he said. "Every meet she was the loudest parent there." Ione taught Tim a nursery rhyme that she repeated often: *Good, Better, Best / Never let it rest / Until your Good is Better / And your Better is Best.*

Tim took the words of his mother's rhyme to heart. He trained hard in the pool. He was a top swimmer in the 400-meter freestyle event. When Tim was 13 years old, his mother found out she had cancer. She received care at the hospital. The care kept her alive.

On September 22, 1989, Hurricane Hugo tore through Saint Croix. The Duncans huddled in a bathroom for five hours. Their solid house survived the storm. But the hurricane crushed many homes and the island's only hospital. Ione could no longer get care from the hospital. The hurricane also destroyed the island's only Olympic-size swimming pool. Tim was forced to practice in the ocean. This frightened him. Tim was afraid of sharks.

Ione's health got worse. She was dying. She made Tim promise to go to college and get a

Hurricane Hugo sank more than 50 boats in the Christiansted Harbor. Others were washed onto the streets.

degree. The day before Tim's 14th birthday, his mother died. Tim was shocked. His birthday came and went without a party. Life for Tim changed. "I understood life and death and everything in between," Tim said. "I understood that I was not going to be around forever."

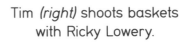

Tim *(right)* shoots baskets with Ricky Lowery.

A Great Thinker

Tim lost interest in swimming. He was about to start ninth grade. His sister Cheryl and her husband, Ricky Lowery, moved into Tim's house. They put up a basketball hoop in the front yard. "Let's shoot a few," Lowery said.

Tim was clumsy at first. He could not run as fast or jump as high as other players.

"I realized that other guys would have more athletic ability than me," Tim said. Lowery taught Tim the proper way to play. Tim learned to dribble on stones and up stairs. He learned to shoot with either hand.

One day in practice, Tim wore his shorts backward by mistake. He had a great practice. Tim has been wearing his shorts backward in practice ever since.

Tim grew eight inches in high school. He became a star player at Saint Dunstan's Episcopal High. He scored about 25 points a game as a senior. Several colleges heard about this thin player who could block shots and rebound. Wake Forest University coach Dave Odom visited Tim. Coach Odom offered him a basketball **scholarship**. At the age of 17, Tim graduated. He was on his way to Wake Forest in North Carolina.

In Tim's first game as a college freshman in 1993, he did not score a point. He was so nervous, he never even took a shot. He soon relaxed and played better. He helped Wake Forest to a 20–11 record.

Playing center his sophomore year, Tim led Wake Forest into the **National Collegiate Athletic Association (NCAA) Tournament**. Tim helped Wake Forest get to the **Sweet 16**. He finished that year with nearly four blocks per game. This was the third most blocks per game in college history. He gave the other teams nightmares. "Every time you turn around, he's staring you in the face," said Missouri forward Derek Grimm. "I could have sworn there were four or five Tim Duncans out there."

Many people said Tim could be the first player selected in the NBA **draft** after just two

Tim scores for
Wake Forest.

years of college. Tim said that
he would stay in school. He chose to
honor his promise to his mother by earning his
degree. As a junior, he scored nearly 20 points
and grabbed more than 12 rebounds per game.
He could have gone to the NBA and earned
millions of dollars. Instead, he stayed at Wake
Forest for his senior year.

Tim was the best player in college during his fourth year at Wake Forest. He was named College Player of the Year. After Tim's final game, his father stood on the court and told the crowd how proud Tim's mother would have been. Then Bill began to say Tim's mother's nursery rhyme, "Good, better, best . . ." Tim hugged his father and stopped him. "That's enough, Dad," he said. Tim is a private man.

Tim brings his father onto the court after Tim's last game with Wake Forest.

The San Antonio Spurs were not a good team before they selected Tim in the draft.

TEAM PLAYER

The San Antonio Spurs chose Tim with the first pick in the 1997 NBA draft. He and the Spurs' **veteran** center David Robinson were called the Twin Towers. Tim proved he was ready for the NBA right away. In one of his first pro games, he grabbed 22 rebounds against the Chicago Bulls.

The Spurs traveled to NBA cities around the country. Tim showed fans his calm style of play. "Emotion doesn't work for me," he explained. "If you show excitement, then you also may show frustration. If your opponent picks up on this frustration, you are at a disadvantage."

Tim led the Spurs to the playoffs in 1998. They beat the Phoenix Suns before losing to the Utah Jazz.

The Spurs faced the Jazz again in the 1999 playoffs. This time, Tim would not allow his team to lose. Near the end of one game, he ripped the ball from superstar Karl Malone and slammed it home. The San Antonio crowd chanted "M-V-P, M-V-P!" Tim heard the chants. "It gave me a tingly feeling," he said.

The Spurs roared through the playoffs,

beating the Minnesota Timberwolves, Los Angeles Lakers, and New York Knicks. The Spurs were the NBA champions! "This is incredible," said Tim. "We kept our focus and pulled it out."

Tim shoots during the NBA Finals.

Tim wears jersey number 21 with the Spurs in honor of Ricky Lowery, his brother-in-law who taught him how to play basketball. Lowery wore that number on his college team.

Players and coaches were in awe. "Words can't even describe the type of player he is," said guard Allen Iverson. Veteran coach Larry Brown said, "He's the ultimate team player. His teammates love him. He's incredible."

Even with all his success, Tim stayed humble. Players tried to rattle Tim with taunts and insults. Tim stayed calm. He studied **psychology** in college. He knew the power of silence. "You absolutely destroy people's minds when you [remain quiet]," he said. "They're talking to you and there's no response other than to make this shot, make this play, get this rebound. People hate that."

Tim holds his first
MVP trophy.

In 2002, Tim set career highs in scoring,
rebounding, **assists**, and **steals**. He was named
MVP of the NBA. But Tim did not care about
winning awards. "If we win, I'm happy," he
said. "The rest of it is just stuff."

The Spurs lost to the Lakers in the playoffs in 2002. Then Tim's father died of cancer. Tim grieved for his dad and worked harder than ever to improve. He won the MVP award again in 2003 and led his team past the Suns, the Lakers, the Dallas Mavericks, and finally the New Jersey Nets, to capture the NBA title. "Tim was astounding in his focus," said Spurs coach Gregg Popovich.

Tim (left) stands with teammate David Robinson after winning the 2003 NBA championship.

Tim *(right)* talks with teammate Tony Parker.

LEADING THE WAY

Tim was given a new role for the 2003–2004 season. David Robinson had retired. Coach Popovich asked Tim to be the team's leader. "I'm a blender, not a leader," Tim replied. But the coach convinced Tim that the team could not win unless he did lead.

Tim moves around a Detroit Pistons defender during the Finals.

Tim did very well in his new role as team leader. The Spurs won the NBA title again in 2005. It took seven games to beat the tough Detroit Pistons in the Finals. "Tim put his team on his shoulders and carried them to a championship," said Pistons center Ben Wallace. "That's what great players do."

Tim struggled through the 2006–2007 season with a painful foot injury. But he recovered in time to lead the Spurs to a fourth championship. He led them to the playoffs again in 2008 and 2009! NBA commissioner David Stern declared, "Tim Duncan is a player for the ages!"

By now, some experts were saying that Tim was the best big man to ever play the game. Coach Popovich simply said, "Very honestly, Tim is not that impressed with himself."

Tim jumps for a layup.

Tim is calm on the basketball court. But off the court, he likes to crack jokes.

Tim is a great player. But just as important, he makes the game fun for his teammates. He passes the ball to them. He praises them and never yells at them. He shows them how to play the right way. "Basketball to some players is physical," says Tim. "To me it's physical and mental. You must not only conquer your opponents physically, you must out-think them. Everything I do is basic, and that doesn't sell. I don't have the icing. My icing is, I just want to win."

Selected Career Highlights

2007-2008   Finished fourth in the NBA in rebounds
Finished eighth in the NBA in blocked shots

2006-2007   Led Spurs to fourth NBA title
Named to All-NBA First Team for the ninth time

2005-2006   Finished fifth in the NBA in rebounds

2004-2005   Led Spurs to third NBA title
Named NBA Finals Most Valuable Player for the third time
Named to All-NBA First Team for the eighth time

2003-2004   Named to All-NBA First Team for the seventh time

2002-2003   Led Spurs to second NBA title
Named NBA Finals Most Valuable Player for the second time
Named NBA Most Valuable Player for the second time
Named to All-NBA First Team for the sixth time

2001-2002   Named NBA Most Valuable Player for the first time
Named to All-NBA First Team for the fifth time

2000-2001   Named to All-NBA First Team for the fourth time

1999-2000   Named NBA Finals Most Valuable Player for the first time
Named NBA All-Star Game Most Valuable Player
Named to All-NBA First Team for the third time

1998-1999   Led Spurs to first NBA title
Named to All-NBA First Team for the second time

1997-1998   First player taken in 1997 NBA draft
Named to All-NBA First Team for the first time
Named NBA Rookie of the Year

1996-1997   Named Naismith College Player of the Year
Named ACC Player of the Year for
  the second time
Named First Team All-America for
  the second time
Led nation in rebounding (14.7 rebounds
  per game)

1995-1996   Named ACC Player of the Year for the first time
Named First Team All-America for the first time

Glossary

assists: passes to teammates that help teammates score baskets

boxes out: a move in which a player uses his or her body to control an area near the basket in preparation for grabbing a rebound

defenders: players who try to stop the other team from scoring

degree: a piece of paper declaring that a person has successfully completed school

draft: a yearly event in which all professional teams in a sport take turns choosing new players from a selected group

dunks: slamming the basketball through the hoop

fouled: to be hit, touched, or pushed in a way that is against the rules

free throws: one-point shots taken from behind the free throw line. Players often get to shoot free throws after being fouled.

layup: a short shot made by placing the ball in the hoop or softly bouncing the ball off the backboard

low post: an area near the basket

National Collegiate Athletic Association (NCAA) Tournament: a yearly tournament in which 65 college teams compete to decide the national champion

playoffs: a postseason tournament held to decide the NBA championship. The NBA playoff system has four rounds. A team must win four games in each round to win the championship.

psychology: the study of the mind, emotions, and human behavior

rebound: to grab the ball after a missed shot

scholarship: an award that helps pay for a student's school fees

steals: plays in which the defender takes the ball from the other team's player

Sweet 16: the last 16 teams competing in the NCAA Tournament

three-point basket: a long-range shot that counts for three points

veteran: a player who has played several years

Further Reading & Websites

Bernstein, Ross. *Shaquille O'Neal*. Minneapolis: Lerner Publications Company, 2009.

Glaser, Jason. *Tim Duncan*. New York: PowerKids Press, 2008.

Kennedy, Mike, and Mark Stewart. *Swish: The Quest for Basketball's Perfect Shot*. Minneapolis: Millbrook Press, 2009.

Roselius, J. Chris. *Tim Duncan: Champion On and Off the Court*. Berkeley Heights, NJ: Enslow Publishers, 2006.

Walters, John. *Tim Duncan*. Chanhassen, MN: Child's World, 2007.

ESPN.com
http://espn.go.com
ESPN.com covers all the major professional sports, including NBA basketball.

Official Site of the San Antonio Spurs
http://www.nba.com/spurs
This official website of the San Antonio Spurs includes the team's schedule and results, late-breaking news, biographies of Tim Duncan and other players, and much more.

Sports Illustrated Kids
http://www.sikids.com
The *Sports Illustrated Kids* website covers all sports, including basketball.

Tim Duncan Official Website
http://www.slamduncan.com
Tim's official website features news, statistics, trivia, and a diary from Tim.

Index

Photo Acknowledgments

The images in this book are used with the permission of: © Dan Anderson/ epa/CORBIS, p. 4; AP Photo/Ann Heisenfelt, pp. 5, 9; AP Photo/Alex Brandon, p. 6; REUTERS/Sean Gardner, p. 8; © Oliver Benn/Stone/Getty Images, p. 10; AP Photo/Steve Helber, p. 13; © Manny Millan/Sports Illustrated/Getty Images, p. 14; AP Photo/Karl DeBlaker, p. 17; AP Photo/Bob Jordan, p. 18; AP Photo/Chuck Burton, p. 19; AP Photo/Ron Frehm, p. 21; AP Photo/Eric Gay, pp. 23, 24, 28; © Paul J. Sutton/Duomo/CORBIS, p. 25; © The Sporting News/ ZUMA Press, p. 26; © Gloria Ferniz/San Antonio Express-News/ZUMA Press, p. 27; © Edward A. Ornelas/San Antonio Express-News/ZUMA Press, p. 29.

Front Cover: © Christophe Elise/DPPI/Icon SMI.